OF

ROOTS & WINGS

AND

HEART-FELT

THINGS

COLLECTED POEMS

BY

JANA CARMAN

Jana Carman

OF

ROOTS & WINGS

AND

HEART-FELT

THINGS

COLLECTED POEMS

BY

JANA CARMAN

ISBN: 9781705917961
Imprint: Independently published

DEDICATED

To St. Davids' Christian Writers
who taught me, critiqued me,
encouraged me, and helped me
spread my writer's wings.

To my parents Doris and Edward Fogg
(see Preface), who laid a foundation
of faith and encouragement.
I know you will meet me at the Door!

To John, the love of my life and
my husband for sixty-plus years;
my first reader, my daily encourager,
and a tireless promoter of my writing.

To John, Pan, and Ginni
who seem happy to be asked
to proof-read, and whose sharp eyes
save me from embarrassing mistakes.

To Leo Thorne, a man of poetry,
whose encouragement blew me away;
and to Shirley, my friend, teacher,
and mentor in the ways of poetry.

To Jonathan Haase whose skillful fingers
and insight designed the cover.

And to my Savior for His
now-and-forever companionship.
How thankful I am for Him!

TABLE OF CONTENTS

Part I

Part II

*See Expanded Contents with titles and page numbers
at back of book*

FOREWORD

Two things children need
to become all they can be:
Roots and Wings

This farmer's daughter was raised close to the soil.
It molded my thinking about true essentials
and formed appreciation for God's beautiful world.
Unlike so many in this restless, uprooted society,
my roots go deep. Seeded by tales of family history,
I grew up into a joyful faith in God.

But more than roots, my parents gave me wings.
Ten years of piano lessons was a gift of music
that still supports me—emotionally and monetarily.
They sent me to college, selling the corn crop
to pay for my second semesters. They freed me
to major in music, never questioning my choice
by saying, "What will you ever use <u>that</u> for?"

And they taught me that words have wings!
Books, books, books! All over the house!
Reading was a magic chariot that whisked us
off to intriguing places—so engrossing
that we would lose track of time.
That's why, in our house, there was a strict rule:

NO READING BEFORE SCHOOL.

And its corollary: **No Reading Before Church!**

Mama's love of reading became a part
of her children, so we all
can soar!

THE QUILT

Life is a patchwork
of roots and wings
of tears and fears
and heartfelt things
of dark-valley days
and mind-blowing joys
of blessed peace
obnoxious noise
hurts and hugs
healing and pain
bane and blessing
loss and gain.

Stitched together with faith
and embroidered with love,
this quilt was personally designed
for me
by God.

PART I.
CHAPTER 1. SEASONS IN POETRY

SPRING

MY NEW YEAR

knows no midnight sleet,
no prism'd glint
from sun-sparked, ice-clad branch.
Instead it greets the greening tree,
bird-song return,
waking earth renewed. Oh yes,
Resurrection had to be in Spring.

SENSING SPRING

Crocuses thrust their stiff green spikes
through the sharp-smelling earth,
watered by the melting snow
that drips in syncopated rhythm
from ice-fringed eaves.

haiku 1

early April breeze
wind-warped tree shivers its leaves
leans toward summer

SURPRISE

Spring seems quietly genteel
with pussy willow grays,
faint reds, pale greens until
bold daffodils and raucous tulips
pop out with a shout.

FOOD FOR THE SOUL

In quest of early lilacs, I
high-stepped across wet lawn
but found my prize already tagged.
Some hunter, nearer dawn
than I, had spread her fragile
dew-pearled trap and caught
a purple plume of fragrant spring.
Not what she'd planned, I thought,
but to my mind a better prey.
I'll take bouquets to bugs
    any day.

MADAM SPIDER

I've worked all night fashioning
my floating field to farm the air.
From deep within myself I spin
my sticky steely silk and shape it,
spoked and netted. Anchored firm,
I sling my seine across the flight paths.
Now I wait.
The early dew embroiders my design;
(a graceful blend-- utility and art,
don't you agree?)
Though Solomon extolled the ant, it's clear
I'm more industrious by far than she:
I weave and trap, cling-wrap my catch
in silk I've manufactured--
Oh!
That's my alarm—excuse me, please.
When something large has landed
I must quickly wrap it lest
its struggles wreck my lovely web
that took all night to weave.

WHAT DO YOU SEE?
In that pale blue bowl above,
ringed with cloud curds,
awash with suds, I see an angel
on kitchen duty "washing up"
the early morning sky.

SPRING EQUINOX
Balanced between
the light and dark,
no more of one than other,
I face the summer of my life.
A child of Light expects to find
more hours of day ahead, and
less of dark—a vernal Christian,
ever-growing, overflowing
into fruitfulness.

MOON-RISE
Beyond the rim of kitchen light,
    familiar scenes lay shadow-changed
    to mystery.
Unstirring limbs and leaves hang etched
    in black against a navy sky,
    and sleepy chirps inquire if Dawn
    will soon arrive.
Not Dawn—another eastern light's
    uncertain shimmer gathers strength
    and rises, spreading silver
    across the water to my feet,
    inviting me to walk
    its path of light.

haiku 2
fragrant foam-tipped waves
offer bouquets to the moon:
mock-orange at night

haiku 3
tree trunks in the mist
materialize below
faded ghostly crowns

OLD ROAD

The new road cuts a shorter path
and we'd almost forgot
that once we went a different way,
a winding beauty spot.
In nostalgia's grip, we trace
once more the older ways,
and memory transports us back,
reliving other days.
The road, well-worn by feet,
by wheels, now is paved with bloom.
The only hint of once-a-road
is where the hedge-rows loom.
Yet not deserted: here in dust
the sparrows' feet print stars,
and tracks of dainty-stepping deer
reveal no fear of cars.
Well, we shall keep our shorter road,
fly by in noise and fumes,
and leave that quiet former path
to birds
and dreams
and blooms.

haiku 4
at country crossroad
traffic light blinks *stop-stop-stop*
frog pauses, blinks back

SUMMER
REGRETS
The remnants of a royal feast
greeted me at dawn.
Like fancy-folded napkins, violets
lay scattered on the lawn.
Were dandelions golden coins
tossed to a troubadour?
Alas, I slept too sound and missed
the ball outside my door.

haiku 5
hanging by one foot
squirrel empties the birdfeeder
while the blue jay scolds

INCENSE
The woods abound with dogwood's bridal white
and mounds of mountain laurel's pale pink blush.
Hedge and road-edge froth with sprays
of honeysuckle and wild rose,
and scent of fresh-cut grass.
I drink it, savor it, and think,
"So must heaven smell to one new-come!
That lily/rose-of-Sharon blend
must be a pure delight to sense long dulled
by earth's corruption and decay."
As odors stir our memories,
may June's incense remind of You,
O my sweet Lord.

haiku 6
leap, twirl, and stagger
all inhibitions dissolved:
filled with the Spirit

LEGERDEMAIN
The pond lies dimpled by the rain,
demure as girls in dotted-swiss array,
until the wind, with airy sleight-of-hand,
transforms it to sophisticate's lamé.

CLOUDBIRTH
Strobes of lightning probe the sky,
thrusting crooked fingers
into the blackness overhead,
gauging the nearness to birth.
The cloud-womb splits: waters break,
cascading, gushing, rushing streams.
(Wipers hurry-scurry, left then right,
their mindless drone a midwife's croon
of "Easy now, Easy now.")
Birthed, expelled, its deluge ebbed,
convulsing still in after-pangs,
the spent storm grumbles distantly.
Gutters gurgle. Trees drip.
And drawing substance from
its parents Earth and Air,
over puddled paths there drifts
the newborn: Mist.

(2nd place Nature poem contest, Parnassus Literary Journal)

MIDAS TOUCH
Rocks viewed
through yellow lenses
seem to glow Midas-touched
and lemon meringue clouds float in
lime skies.

(This is a cinquain, a five line stanza with syllable count: 2,4,6,8,2.)

SUMMER EVE
In the twilight fireflies blink
in cold-light code:
Here I am, here I am.
Intercepted, captured,
and imprisoned,
they flash their SOS
to those still free
until their sparks go out.

TAKE-OFF
The firefly's afterburner
rockets him upward
after each cold-light signal.

ENDANGERED SPECIES
(A young girl once told me:)
"There's plenty of fireflies.
What does one matter
if I smear its cool light in my palm?"

If so, we might say:
There's plenty of rabbits
and stray dogs and cats.
If they're out in the road—well, too bad.
There's plenty of babies.
Hey, that I don't need!
Frankly, I've other plans for my life.
There's plenty of old folks.
If they're hogging resources
and are useful no more—pull the plug.
Yes, there's plenty of species.
Yet of all those endangered,
I think we'll miss most
the tender of heart.

SCIENCE AND SONG
Let science say
that lyric flute-like note
that flows from thrush's pulsing throat
merely marks in melody
"These woods are mine" –
an avian 'No Trespass' sign.

Let science say a mother's lullaby
is music's mimicry
of heartbeat, nine months long;
and memory (subliminal)
is that which soothes in song.

And let scientists propound
(if they must) that lust
is all that makes the world go round;
that God is only Nature's other name,
(whatever theologians claim).
That "music of the spheres"? Hyperbole,
not celestial harmony.

New science often proves
past "science" wrong.
Some day they may discover
what the birds knew all along—
a world of love and mystery
gives rise to song.

FAITH AND HEALING
Beyond the brazen serpent-rod *
Faith sees, and seizes,
the power of God.

Numbers 21:8,9

RAINY DAY ACTIVITY

The first few drops hesitate,
then hustle in a sudden spate
down the glass. With each pass
they lay transparent trails
    (not quite like snails;)—
these riverbeds an eighth-inch wide
guide each drop from top
to windowsill, then spill
in tiny waterfalls down walls
and onto thirsty flowers.
    Caged by this sudden shower, I race
the raindrop rivulets, and trace,
one-fingered, here inside the pane
my *dry* path mirroring the rain.
    (Adults don't do such things.
When I'm caught, this grownup laughs,
pretending she was merely
wiping smudges off the glass.)

KITE

Poems are kites
earth-tied
air-borne
tugging at both ends.

TRANSITORY GLORY

Along the road day-lilies grow.
Each regal trumpet sways
on slender stem a single day.
Tomorrow finds it limp,
collapsed, soon dying.
But today,
with orange hearts a-blaze,
along the road day-lilies glow.

HIDE AND SEEK

Late June, and twilight seems to stretch
on and on and on,
punctuated by lightning bugs
and children's calls:
"Here I come, ready or not.
Anyone 'round my base is It."

I crouch beneath a bush,
mock-orange sweetness vying
with the dusty smell of earth.
Above my head, the grownups' talk
and laughter trickles through
the screen and down across
the crickets' song.

The time before, I hid behind
the rambler rose. I lick a scratch.
It tastes of blood and dust, and just
a little, of adventure.
Eight is young to brave the dark.
Inside, steps tip-tap across the floor.
"Come on in. It's much too dark
to play outside," my mother calls.

Too dark to play? Too dark to spy
my hiding place! It must be so—
they hadn't found me yet.
So, torn between the scary fun
of night-time hide-and-seek
and lighted windows' welcoming,
with dragging feet, we heed her call.
Here we come,
ready or not.

MICROCOSM
When the tide retreats,
microcosmic oceans
stay behind, reflecting
in their sandy basins
dime-size suns
or even oceans, drier,
bluer, wider, deeper,
more unforgiving
than wildest writhing water.
We two walk the shore
discovering
universes in puddles.

UNEASY CO-EXISTENCE
I am a mole
I do mole-ish things
I tunnel here and there
harvesting my grassroots' feast
of grubs beneath the giants' heavy tread
and tiptoeing of cats
I only do
what all moles always do
Why then should cats
lie in wait
and humans stomp
my cozy tunnels flat?
I am a mole
and I do mole-ish things
So I wonder—is that
a human thing they do?

WILLOW
I am willow
rooted by the stream,
graceful in storm or calm,
haven to small birds
and small boys.
Some call me "dirty tree"
for my litter of twigs.
"Damn tree" others fume
when my roots, seeking water,
invade their wells and pipes.
"Dancing tree," "dreaming tree,"
"delightful tree" say those
who feel my grace and beauty
transcends practicality.

TREE-CUTTING
The curious count the rings;
the soulful mourn the slaughter;
the business-minded calculate
how many feet of prime lumber
for backyard decks or picnic tables
can be harvested from
this fallen monarch of the woods.

What will this world be like
when these young saplings, planted now,
rear heads as high as those
now stretched out on the ground?
Will there be man to view in awe,
or come to plunder once again
what took millennia to grow?

AUTUMN

ACROPHOBIA

I don't want to know
what lies ahead, or far below.
God guides each step and holds my hand
so I may safely, calmly stand
on danger's edge or pleasure's shore,
content and trusting ever more
my loving Guide, my God.

MAKE ME AN INSTRUMENT

I am a tool, designed
for a special purpose.
A mop
may serve as a door-stop
but a scalpel is wasted
as a letter opener.
Use me, Lord,
as you designed me.
Make me an instrument
of your Peace.

Too long have I lived among those who hate peace.
I am a man of peace, but when I speak, they are for war.
Psalm 120:6,7

WHERE THERE IS HATRED . . .

And where is it, *not*?
Road rage flares hot.
Nations and races
nurse old wrongs,
draw apart in distrust.
Hate is a bane that poisons life.
(Could there be an antidote?)

COMPLACENCY

We live a quiet life,
   a life where Nature is our friend
   and seasons turn without an end
   from hot to cold, and back again
      in peaceful wheel.
For we have never known
   our hills to vomit out their life
   in flaming stream, nor earthquake's knife
   that severs house from house, nor strife
      of mushroom'd war.
We cannot comprehend
   a world bare-stripped, all death and rust,
   laid waste by fire and poisoned dust,
   a blackened, ruined, hostile crust
      unfit for man.
Complacently we live,
   believing what has not yet passed
   will never come,
   and peace will last,
      world without end.

And then – September 11, 2001 . . .

"Disaster will strike them without warning
and they will be fatally wounded." Proverbs 6:11 TEV

. . . . The antidote for Hate
   fills my sower's pouch.
      Let me sow Kindness,
         let me sow Love.

May there be peace within your walls
and security within your citadels.
For the sake of my brothers and friends, I will say,
Peace be within you." Psalm 122:7,8

SKY-WATCH, 2001

The sky was strangely empty—
only birds and wisps of cloud
dotted that autumn blue
un-streaked by jet trails.
    Had we not watched as planes
brought down skyscrapers,
this silence and this emptiness
might be pre-Kitty Hawk.
    Then, overhead, droned one lone plane,
south-bound. With re-stirred fear we saw it
U-turn in the sky, and thought
of a Pennsylvania field strewn
with pieces of plane and people.
    Seeing the fear in each other's eyes,
we feebly joked, "Guess he forgot
his lunch. Or . . ." Our voices trailed off.
    I checked the TV news for several days.
No news is good news—so they say.

HEART HARMONICS

The evening news may make me cry.
Just so,
the crystal vase on my piano
sings in sympathy
with some struck chord.

WHERE THERE IS DESPAIR . . .

Despair oozes in like sewage
seeping into a well,
dispersing its contaminants,
sickening the will.
The remedy is Hope.

CLIMB THE ROPE

Enveloped by despair,
we drop into a deep, dark well.
From there, stars' faint gleams
are seen, forever out of reach.
Hope is a rope
let down from above.
We only need to grab it
to be pulled up
into the sunshine.
Glorious, strong and shining,
hope affirms: with God
all is well, and ever will be.
He is our Hope.

WHERE THERE IS DARKNESS . . .

Few things thrive in dark,
and fewer yet are good.
Fungi come to mind—mushrooms,
but also athlete's foot.
Light invigorates, heals
and draws growth up towards itself.

TOUCHÉ

My touch-on lamp
blinks into light
at passing trains
or power surge from
lightning strikes.
I'm wondering—
what does it take
to jar *me* awake?
What bolt from the blue
ignites you?

WAFFLE WEATHER

Before the power company poles
came marching past the farms,
our windmill welcomed every breeze
like me—with open arms.
      Blow, wind, blow.
      I long for waffle weather.

Mama told me sailors whistled
up a wind to fill their sail.
But tweet and pucker though I might,
I blew to no avail.
      Blow, wind, blow.
      Bring me waffle weather.

Delco batteries fed our lights,
but waffle-making waited
for stronger current, which the blur
of windmill indicated.
      Spin, windmill, spin.
      Cranked up by waffle weather.

Today it's easy to have waffles
anytime you crave.
Take them from the freezer, serve them
piping hot from microwave.
      Tasty, yes, light as a feather.
      But—where's the taste of waffle weather?

TIME AND AGAIN

clock hands meet
neatly scissor time
Now becomes Past

COUNTRY QUIET

Late night silence sings its country song
with ticking clock and old-house creaks.
A nearby owl in sycamore repeats
Hoo, hoohoo, hoo, hoohoo,
not waiting in between
for owl's reply from distant tree.
The furnace in the cellar sulks.
Though fall is here, the price of oil reminds
of last year's budget crunch, and so
we tough it out, the thermostat set low.
Quiet settles like a quilt,
no cars go humming down the road,
and, like mosquitoes, *tinnitis*
forever buzzes in my brain.
Peace blankets the house.
I sink into sleep.

AUTUMN PRAYER

Frost lays light fingers on my life,
its cool touch welcome after fevered days.
To sun's foreshortened rays
my leaves respond, begin to blaze,
reflect a far greater Sun,
and lift my heart to praise.

EPITAPH

The fall leaves die in glory,
lifting hearts to praise.
So, in the sight of God,
the death of those He loves
is precious, beautiful,
a lovely end to days,
and prelude to eternity.

SPLIT INFINITUDE

When an acorn splits,
an oak starts to grow.
When a sunbeam splits,
a rainbow appears.
When an atom splits,
great power is released.
So,
what marvelous thing can He make
when a soul
abandons itself
to His chisel?

PRUNING

Anticipating future springs,
but still in winter's grip,
my trees need pruning.
I need a lopper and a mental view
of what is best for good tree growth.
First, discard all rotten wood,
each crossed and rubbing branch,
and open up the center to the sun.
Cut out the weak and prune the strong
to shape it for healthy bearing.
(The pile of discards sometimes seems
to rival the remaining tree, but
pruning will encourage growth.)
Anticipating heaven,
though still in earth's cold grip,
my soul needs pruning, too.

haiku 7

rivers of blackbirds
stream southward to winter home
farewell until spring

winter

WINTER MORNING
Low sun paints stripes of green
across the frosty grass.
Dead reeds glint with false life
and sway in the fitful breeze.
Far-off dogs, south-bound geese,
the neighbor's rooster,
all sound close, and icy air
tickles inside my nose.

haiku 8
winter morning fog
frozen like fine lace on twigs
glitters in cold sun

9
snow geese on the wing
squadrons and wedges and strings
scribbled on the sky

10
overhead, snow geese
wings shimmer like illusions
honks shatter the spell

WINTER BALLET
Snowflakes pirouette
down the morning air. Then
lifted by invisible partners
they tease the eye into believing
it's snowing . . . downside-up.

FIRST SNOW

The thermometer nudges 20,
my breath hangs in a cloud.
Deer tracks along the road
are struck deep in frozen mud.
Hands a-fist in mittens and
arms a-swing, I beat
myself for warmth.
Turning homeward, an icy wind
stings my face, waters eyes,
sets my nose a-drip.
A snow-dusted cedar sports
a patch of cardinal's scarlet.
Peeking through a tall pine,
the sun silvers branches, dazzles eyes.
Home is in sight, and welcoming.
I stomp up the walk, already
feeling warmed by thoughts
of oatmeal with cream, hot cocoa,
and warm woolen socks.

SNOW JOB

Fresh snow fell last night
covering the dirty mess
of yesterday:
the scrapings of the road,
papers, cans and bottles
which never fully come to light
until spring thaw.
A snow job –so like all
my attempts at self-reform,
clean layered over garbage,
mere temporary gain
until the day the Son's eyes
will melt all disguise.

SNOW
Descending gently
Delicate artistry
Infinite variety
Hexagonal intricacy
Myriad individuality
Fingerprints of Deity

WINTER FIREFLIES
Storm drain, waste water steam,
common weeds along the road,
bitter frosty night—unlikeliest
components for delight.

Fragile stems ice-diamond'd
by steam, stroked by headlights
into scintillating life:
Oh look!
a cloud of phantom fireflies
dancing in the winter night!

*A reminder that winter beauty can have
its dangerous side.*

SNOW-ANGEL DANGER
False warmth chills
and fills with deadly drowze
the child who nestles,
languid, lost, and drained of tears,
in nature's frigid featherbed;
all unaware Snow-angel's
colder twin, Death-angel,
masquerades as Sleep
and stalks these winter woods.

CHAPTER 2. MAY I INTRODUCE . . . ?

Myself: I AM FROM

I am from
  the garden part of the Garden State,
  with farms and muskrat marshes,
  where meadow mud between your toes
  means you'll never leave
  (or at least, always come back).
I am from
  the backwoods end-of-the-world
  where dark and narrow roads are named
  Hell Neck, Frog Ocean, Battercake Lane;
  people live on "Necks" of land between
  creeks named Alloways, Mad Horse, Stow.
I am from
  low-lying marshy land you cannot leave
  without crossing a bridge or two,
  gas and food stores are a ten-mile drive,
  and nothing impedes the glorious view
  of sunsets, sunrises, star-spangled sky.
I am from
  a community where most are related,
  and some, though residents for fifty years,
  are outsiders still; a place where life's pace
  is more 1930 than 2000-plus,
  despite satellite dishes on each house.
I am from
  farm-rooted, church-grounded,
  meadow-muddied, mosquito-inoculated,
  ancestor-aware stock. No matter where I roam,
  that meadow mud between my toes
  draws me back to where
              I am from.

MAMA'S LEGACY

She had an eye for all the loveliness
of nature's sea and sky and fields;
an ear to musical delights
and poems' inner pace and sense;
a love of books whose endless joys
supply both facts and insights gleaned
from other people's hearts and minds;
a sense of fun and humor—spice
for seasoning the daily grind;
the joy of doing many things
and pride in doing well;
a moral compass, Bible-based;
and best of all, a lived-out faith
in Christ, the Hub and Anchor
of her joyful Christian life.

"Her children arise, and call her blessed; . . .
Charm is deceptive, and beauty is fleeting,
but a woman who fears the Lord
is to be praised." Proverbs 31:29,30

BOUQUET À PROPOS

Fooled by the mild December sun
into a winter bloom,
Louisa's ancient quince asserts
the calendar is wrong.
    Three sprigs, a last bouquet, are tucked
between her stiffly folded hands.
Two of a kind: the spiky quince
and Louisa, who at ninety-three
was sharp and spunky, full of life
right to the final plucking.

SILENT WORSHIP

To those who cannot hear,
you speak
with hands like fluttering birds,
thoughts sketched
in dancing shorthand
on the stained-glass air.
In graceful unrhymed rhythm
(like blank verse in motion)
you translate sound to sight.
Your silent hallelujahs rise
like prayers,
like incense
shimmering the air.
Fingers flick a quick-
spelled word, then stroke
unspoken benedictions
over silent worshipers.
I love the singing sounds of words,
but you, with speaking hands,
make music for my eyes.
(Dedicated to interpreters for the deaf)

WIDOW'S WALK

I noticed those two trees before,
so closely grown they looked like one.
Now one has toppled in a storm
and one remains. The roots
still twine deep where I cannot see,
but branches dangle, broken when
it tried to check its partner's fall.
It stands forlorn, just half a tree.
    I came back from my lonely walk
into these lonely rooms,
and felt afresh the pain and chill
on my bare side where once you stood.

TO GRANDMOTHER

You seemed so old to my young eyes,
so stern, unlike my mother;
so busy as you cooked each day
for family and hired men.
For more-than-ample meals, you baked
molasses cakes and homemade bread.
Hands ever busy, but mind well-read.
And now when it's too late
to say that I appreciate
the Christmas books and overnights
(with owls for lullabies),
now I look back and fondly see
how patient you were, training me
to fill the wood-box, close the gate,
and scrub the walk of "chicken's messin'."
You loved me as you did my braids
and checked my ears and lessons.

Since my 'thanks' comes *years* too late,
I guess I'll have to try to be
the special kind of grandmother
you always were to me.

INTRUDER

Brown-spotted, veined
and knuckle-gnarled—
whose hands, pray tell,
are these?
They can't belong
to one so young,
but they're sticking out
my sleeves.

SEMPER PARATUS?

I'm careful, foresighted,
always prepared—
pen and pad by the phone,
four tires and a spare,
guestroom bed made up,
Blue Shield and Blue Cross,
insured house and car,
life and limb, fire or loss.
I've a Triple A card,
MasterCard and a VISA.
I buy food in bulk
and keep meals in the freeza.
Though I'm ready for anything
common or rare,
do I entertain angels
at times
unaware?

ONLY FIFTY

Some say
that fifty's far too old
for midnight strolls,
impassioned love,
and barefoot picnicking.
But *I* say:
given a youthful heart
and eager mind,
fifty's almost too young!
. . . All right,
 I'll put my shoes back on.
But I'm still
seventeen inside!

APPLE PHILOSOPHER

Well, boy, some men choose their women
just like folks choose apples:
if it's shiny, with an elegant shape—
no matter what it's like inside nor
what it's good for—that's what they grab.
I 'spose that's why the Red Delicious
is America's favorite apple.
Sure ain't mine.
Give me an old-fashioned Winesap
or an Idared. Nothing much
to look at, but taste it fresh,
and your juices start to run!
Crisp and tart, it makes you wish
October lasted all year long.
Women and apples go way back,
to the first garden, some say.
I do think it was an apple
Eve gave to ole Adam.
Although it might a' been a peach,
the apple gets my vote.
I'm partial to 'em. Raised 'em now
for forty years and more.
Now take one of them Blushin' Golds—
men prefer blonds, they say,
but that don't go for apples.
Yellows don't sell near like reds.
They're often better keepers, though.
This one stays firm and tasty long past
when some more preferred ones
shrivel up and dry.
Here, son, try this one for taste.
That's an Arkansas Black.
I bet you never woulda guessed
it would taste that good
with that funny color skin.   *(continued*

I tell you, boy, it's never wise
to choose your apples
or your friends
(or women, for that matter)
by just their looks.
What counts is what's inside—
   every time.
   Every time!

I REMEMBER

I remember
 a wall of windows whose shades
 drew from top as well as bottom,
 the coal-guzzling monster in winter
 that would roast "near-bys"
 and barely warm the corners.
I remember
 Lincoln and Washington
 flanking the flag and clock,
 underscored by Palmer's
 Handwriting System cards.
I remember
 Mrs. Miller's gentle tact
 as she offered old-fashioned bloomers
 to replace the panties I'd wet
 from being too new, too scared
 to ask permission to go
 to the "basement."
I remember
 my very first teacher
 with love.

TO A DEAR OLD LADY

"She shows her age," one said of you.
In fond defense, I thought, *How few
at half her age look half so fine!*

I guess the mounting years do show
in sags and creaking joints, although
this evidence of passing time
my loving heart sees, less as part
of age, and more as antique charm.

Who loved the youthful you as I
do now? Did they, too, wish to buy
you gifts but found their pockets bare?
Who found you welcoming at dusk,
alight and warm? Or did they just
take for granted you were there?

If so, dear Home, * I hope you know
that now, old though you be,
you're dearly loved by me.

** My family home, the William Bradway house,
built 1701.*

THE RAISIN

A raisin—last year's grape
sun-dried for durability,
unspoiled/unspoiling,
sweetness intensified;
good at all times,
available year-round,
concentrated value,
and easy to indulge in:
My sun-kissed father.

PORTRAIT

Gather words to paint her likeness,
words of character and trait:
candid, humorous, and helpful,
vigorous, articulate.
Gather objects: three-tined forks,
duck-wing dusters, home-squeezed juice,
sunbonnets, overalls, and hammocks,
butter paddles (with *double* use!)
Gather humorous turns of speech:
funny made-up names for folk,
"That's the time!" and "antymires";
frankness—what she thought, she spoke.
Gather incidents like: Cowtown
("best for hamburg") every week;
organist or paperhanger; while
reading aloud, she'd fall asleep.
Gather kitchen specialties:
coconut cake, high and white,
cup-custard in the gravy bowl,
baked beans for Saturday night.
Gather things she likes: canaries,
violets, the color blue,
eating, reading, plants, and hymns
(she's a constant hummer too.)
One's personality is sketched
by more than features, hair and eyes.
It's drawn by living—words and deeds. **Presenting:
ETHEL DILKS! Surprise!**

*Written at the family's request
for Mrs. Dilks' 80th birthday celebration.*

AWOL

When men kill
and kill
and kill
and gun barrels scorch
their shaking hands
and buddies' dying
screams echo
endlessly
in blast-deafened ears
and the rich red tide of life
fountains, ebbs and dyes
green uniforms and black alike—
a mind goes AWOL
from too much
death, too close
horror, too long

the eyes are windows
in an empty house

This was written about a photo of a soldier with what was called Shell Shock in previous wars; now PTSD.

DEFENSE TACTIC

My mind a battleground can be
where Satan, direst enemy,
by bold assault or ambush, may
attack, or drain my peace away.
But two can play that warring game.
My best defense is Jesus' name.

ESTRANGED

Can you who savored once
the feast of fellowship
be satisfied with husks
to eat and Grace to sip?
Does not your heart remember, yearn
for days of Love and Grace
when you and He together walked?
You sought His loving face,
delighted in His company,
rejoiced to do His will—
but now you shun His presence, raise
heart-barricades.
              Yet still
He is the same: the faithful Friend,
Companion, Father, Guide.
He longs for you. Estrangement hurts
Him, too! Must wounded pride
keep you apart, or failure's guilt?
The Father pleads: "Restore
to Me the child I love, to you
the joy you knew before.
Run to my arms and gladden both
our hearts once more."

GRAFFITI

Written large,
written small,
boldly splashed
across the sky,
or painted on the heart,
are words the world
can't scrub out:
Jesus loves you.

PAST PERFECTION

She'll sure find things to fuss about
in heaven— the angels sing too loud,
her halo tends to tarnish, or
the golden street hurts her feet.
Little suited Lil. Did you know
she painted over a stained-glass window?
The green, she thought, looked better brown. *

I never left the house quite sure
I looked all right. She'd twitch my tie
or tut-tut at a spot I'd swear
no human eye but hers could see.
Every morning of my life
she sent me off to work unsure.
I'd check the mirror, try all day
to spy what she had seen a-miss.

I 'spose I'll come to sloven's ways.
She always said I'd be a slob
without her there to jack me up.
It's a relief, I can't deny,
to have her gone. When nothing ever suits,
it's mighty hard to bear Perfection
constantly in search of fault.

*Our last parsonage had two lovely stained-glass windows over
the stairway. One day as I passed a window I noticed a brown
section had a scratch across it, revealing green underneath.
I spent hours carefully scratching off the brown overlay
from each window.
I don't know who was responsible for the "paint job" so this
poem is my idea how it may have happened.*

INUNDATED

Who would have thought
a few kind words
would breach the dam
that years had formed
around her hurt? Waist-deep
and nearly whelmed with words,
I fought to keep my feet
against her flood of memories.
Unsure just what had loosed the tide,
with half-learned skills I tried
to see a pattern in the waves of pain,
to probe the depths
and find the source.
That spring of discontent
had seeped and oozed for years
until today, when sympathy
undammed the bitter torrent of
her hoarded tears.

BRAVE AND BEAUTIFUL

* Vashti, summoned,
refused to come.
* * Esther, her successor,
came unsummoned.
Two queens, both beautiful,
both brave, both willing
to risk everything
for principle.

Xerxes was richer
than he knew.

* Esther 1:12   *** Esther 4:11; 5:1,2*

CHAPTER 3. HOMESPUN PHILOSOPHY

DISCORD AND RESOLUTION

Where hand-in-hand we two once walked,
we wander, separately, this maze
of walls we've built of hurt and rage.
Our harsh words clash and ricochet
off endless bitter barricades.
Could I but find the barest breach,
thrust through that hole my hand
and feel yours grasping mine again,
we'd see these walls disintegrate.
We can, together, make a gate.
Love, here's my hand.
Where's yours?

FENCES, WALLS AND GATES

Walls and fences separate—
forbidding, high,
razor-wire topped,
gated communities,
even cozy picket fences
knee-deep in flowers.
Walls and fences enclose—
guard rails, swimming pools,
"invisible fences" for dogs.
We build walls and fences,
huddle inside, separate
and safe (so we think).
But mostly
what we need are gates.
That well-worn path to a gate
between neighbors is paved
(invisibly) with friendship.

NOVA

No more shall Sun be light by day,
no more bright Moon by night.
Your God shall be your glory; aye,
and everlasting Light.
No shadows cast—nor could there be
some lurking dusky corner where
all-present Light can't see!
(Isaiah 60:19 paraphrased)

haiku 11

few things thrive in dark
but—light invigorates, heals
drawing growth upward

LIGHT AND DARK PERSPECTIVE

Light can bless —or blind — unshaded eyes.
But shadow, as the artist knows, adds
semblance of life — depth and shape.
We speak of Rembrandt and Kinkade
whose painted light arrests the eye.
Yet darkness is the foil, the frame,
that underscores the contrast.

The Sun of Righteousness once rose
upon our sadly-shadowed world.
Had all been light before, we might
have deemed His Light unneeded, even dim.
Our need, our darkness, even our sin
is silhouetted by His Glory.
Like moths, we're drawn to His Light
where He sculpts us full-rounded
in His image. Then, as before
(that finishing touch) He breathes
into His new creation:
Life

A PARADOX :

SCULPTOR

Each is a tool in his own hands,
a character to shape
and smooth, or else deface.
From God comes Plan
and clay (or rock),
and by his deeds
Man sculpts himself.
My actions sign my work
and advertise
"a self-made man."

SCULPTED

I lie, unformed, in Potter's hands.
My character He shapes
through circumstance and test,
His Son the Prototype
and I the blank
from which He plans to sculpt
a replica, and mark
me with His brand:
"a God-made man."

BALANCE SHEET

Judged by my production:
  how many meals fixed, beds made,
  rooms cleaned, jars canned,
  lessons taught, money earned.
    Quantity measured by inch and cup.
Assess my worth by:
  lives touched, children nurtured,
  souls comforted, saints taught,
  spouse encouraged, happiness spread.
    Quality measured by eternity.

"Without resistance you can do nothing." Jean Cocteau

BEFORE THE WIND

Helpless as a floating leaf,
my vessel, lacking steerageway,
answers not her helm, but yaws
and drifts, drawn by the urgent tide
toward certain wreck. But when I drop
the centerboard of will, pull up
the flapping canvas of my faith
to catch the wind that whispers hope
to waiting mast, the Spirit
bellies out the sail and bears
my craft against the tide.

PIPES OF PEACE

In Rembrandt's shadowed room
his painted smokers sit
in shafts of sun
and puff in peace
their long curved pipes.
Half a world away,
faint light flickers,
firefly-like,
on dark-bronze skin
as each in turn draws deep,
passes on the pipe
of peace.
Hope's eternal embers glow
though peace
may shift like smoke.

GROWING PAINS

I've grown in body, yet I find
myself still chained to childish ways:
Old habits fettering my mind.
Growing means the Old won't fit,
and like new shoes, the New,
so stiff at first, may chafe a bit.

Still, it's worth the pain to hear
the Father say with joyous tones,
"Good gracious, child,
look how you've grown!"

AN OUTGROWN HIDEAWAY
(for Brian Z.)

Little cabin in the woods,
relic of a boyhood phase,
as you were built, you taught me much
of boys' and grownups' varied ways:
some persevere (their dream is strong),
some slack as other interests swell.
(Little cabin in the woods,
did you know you'd taught so well?)

Many thrive on busyness and noise,
some few, like me, love solitude.
Thanks for times you offered me
a refuge or calm interlude.

Your age is showing. I suppose
someday you'll slowly fall apart;
but memories that I've built of you
are solid structures in my heart.

CHAPTER 4. THE WRITING EXPERIENCE

CONNECTING

You can write a poem
about anything
dusting   dancing   dying
making bread
making money
making love
a stone in your shoe
a spear in your side
gold   or   God   or   gingerbread
fireworks   fireflies   fireplaces
far-off burning constellations
maps   moss   hot cross buns
old cold hates
recipes   racism
altars   ants   abattoirs
With my poem I throw
a line across the gulf
between two minds, saying
"Do you feel this too?"

DISTRACTION RE-VALUED

A too-enthusiastic squirt—
and tiny rainbows rise and float,
detergent bubbles drift across
the soaking pot where oatmeal burned
while Inspiration snared my thoughts.
On the rug the vacuum waits
while rainbows in the kitchen sink
distract my mind with poetry.

RHYME-TIME IN THE KITCHEN
Poems, like children, often pick
an inconvenient time
to insist I take them up, embrace
and set them down in rhyme.
At times I've brushed one off: "Not now,
I'm busy, can't you see?"
then found, when I had time for it,
it had no time for me.
I've learned when poems interrupt,
to welcome, not repel,
and hope, while inspiration burns,
the roast won't burn as well.

WOUND WRAPS
Forgiveness often comes unstuck
and peels away, uncovering the hurt.
(I catch myself picking at the edge. . . .)
I need to use a better brand,
the kind that Jesus used:
stuck on with love and not
removed to check how far
the healing has progressed.
Unless it's held there firmly by the will,
forgiveness that's no more than feeling
won't result in lasting healing.

UN-AUTHORIZED
I'm flattered, and really not vain,
and I honestly hate to complain
that my poem is in print,
but you gave me no hint,
and it's not yet in public domain.
Sent to an editor, who was not amused!

QUICKSILVER RE-VERSED

A fumble, and the fragile form
lies shattered. Drops divide,
driblets subdivide and slide
skitter-scattering
from a heavy-handed touch.

Pushing shards aside, once more
I try to nudge the nubs
of quicksilver/thought together,
gently, delicately, and -- yes!
Mysteriously they coalesce
into a single silvery whole.

Mercury is like my Muse:
though never one to be coerced,
yet now and then
it can be coaxed.

ON HOLY GROUND

Creative God, Your gift
comes blowing through my mind.
It burns within,
demanding only
that I acknowledge
Who You are
and whence
my inspiration comes.
May I not stand
bathed in its flickering glow,
still   stubbornly   shod.

*"Take off your sandals, for the place where you are standing
is holy ground." Exodus 3:5*

MY THESAURUS

I finger my gold,
fondle my jewels,
gloat over their splendor,
love their liquid whispering
      (crystal . . . silver . . . Chantilly)
feel the soothing of my spirit
      (cozy . . . firelight . . . featherbed)
or the stirring of my blood
      (swashbuckling . . . derring-do)
I test their mettle
      (courage . . . passion . . . integrity)
and find they all ring true.

After choosing carefully
which ones to spend, I close
my Treasure Chest, slide
it back in its accustomed niche
between Webster's Dictionary
and Writer's Market Guide.

POETRY CLASS

With chairs pulled up in pairs and threes,
we read our homework poem aloud
with outward calm but inward fears,
our stomachs filled, it seems, with bees.
Exposed by what we write, half-proud,
half-scared, and sometimes close to tears.

Rhyme pattern: ABCABC

DRAWN FROM THE SPRING

Far from here and now, some small idea
once fell on fertile soil and made its way,
first underground, then trickling down
across the years, through midnight channels
of my mind.
          Until today.   Just now
it surfaced, seeking outlet, flooding
line by line across my page.
     My first concern is bottling it in words;
later comes analysis: Does it flow?
Has it depth? Is it murky? Or obscure?
Did I muddle what I meant to say—
too wordy, clouding clarity?
     Poems are formed of effervescence
firmed to sounds, refreshing, yet
non-filling. But far from quenching thirst,
a taste of poetry only seems to whet
the appetite for more.

STAINED GLASS WINDOW

Tiny splintered bits of glass
are sorted by the Master's hand.
Only He knows how these shards
and scraps fit in His plan.
Bit by bit the work takes shape,
chaos surrenders to design.
Still it won't spring into life
'til lit and pierced by
God's sunshine.
Beauty from ashes,
glory from dust.
This splendor all began
with tiny broken pieces
and His Master Plan!

POETIC LARCENY

"Come share my pleasant stones."
This gypsy line haunts me.
Is that some other poet's line,
or mine, my gift, a present
from my Muse that sparks a poem,
and without which the words
lie leaden on the page?

It resonates within my mind,
and yet —I hesitate.
Could this be poet's equivalent
of stealing jewels? Or may I claim
this line of simple words as free
and shining as the sun's gold rain?

There is an incongruity
I can't escape that this, the line
that speaks of generosity
should be the one I long to steal.
(I shudder at my guilt revealed:
Am I a secret thief of words?)

INFERTILITY

Like fond new mothers, poet friends
display their work. "I write a poem
every day, a sonnet twice a week."
Another claims, "My poems come in spates."
I smile (mere stretch of lip), congratulate
their quiver-ful of work, and wonder
barrenly, what closed my womb
to literary offspring. Why,
I pray, why have I
left off bearing?

BUILDING WORD CASTLES

Some hew their words
     precisely
         lay them up
              straight side to side
        so, like the pyramids
     or Solomon's Temple
no cracks are visible.

No mortar used
     could hold their blocks
         more tightly than
             their mounded weight
                already does.
My words
        drift
           off
unless I anchor them
in rhythm, adding here
and there a trowel-ful
of rhyme.

BIRD IN HAND

Ideas hop, like pigeons,
just out of reach
upon my mental windowsill.
Quick!
Snatch that unwary thought
and pen it in a cage of lines
and paragraphs, or rhymes.
(Yet seldom is the bird I've caught
quite so brilliant as I thought.)

TORNADO
Men spoke [wrote] from God as they were carried along by the Holy Spirit. 2 Peter 1:21 NIV

Picked up by the Spirit's whirlwind
I gasp and fight for breath as He
blows me off my calculated course
and sets me gently down
in an unexpected place.
Smoothing my ruffled hair
and dignity, I find (once more)
He's dropped me in the perfect spot—
a larger task than I had planned *
but one that we, together,
(God and I)
can weather.

* *This describes my experience in writing books.*

IN THE BEGINNING
A mighty Word was spoken,
        its rolling sound evoking
                into being everything.
Echoes will reverberate
    along the corridors of time
    and even through eternity,
            telling of God's consummate
                verbal creativity.

BILLBOARD
The Word was nailed up,
poster for the world to read:
"I love you." Signed, God

PUNCTUATION POEMS:

THE APOSTROPHE '
The apostrophe
never puts its foot down
but hovers
possessively
at word's end, a hummingbird
whose wing-beats blur
to invisibility
as it
so delicately
connects.

(PARENTHESES)
Parentheses
stride bowlegged
(like a cowboy)
into sentences,
interrupting
with nonessentials
but adding color.
(Yippee!)

? SPANISH/ENGLISH ?
Spanish warns you up front
of the shift from declarative
to interrogative,
then reverses at the end,
just as questions
reverse the direction
of conversation's flow.
Smart idea.
? Si ?

CHAPTER 5. MUSIC'S MANY FORMS

PSALM FOR THE 21ST CENTURY
1. Praise the Lord.
   Praise God in his infinite universe;
   praise him in his infinitesimal microcosms.
2. Praise him for his diversity;
   praise him for his constancy.
3. Praise him with the chaining of synapses;
   praise him with motion and emotion.
4. Praise him with exuberance and dancing;
   praise him with awe and bent knee.
5. Praise him with the sounds of bells and guitars;
   praise him with resounding pipe organs.
6. Let everything that has breath praise the Lord.
   Praise the Lord! O praise the Lord!

WORSHIP STYLES
Stradivarius
worshiped through wood;
Michelangelo
with paint and stone.
Bach's worship flowed
through pipes and strings,
(and mine, with hands on keys).

This world still cherishes
their violins, statues, ceilings, music.
Although the minds and fingers
are long-since faded into dust,
the song
lingers on.

CREATION MUSIC

When triune God sang, "Let there be . . . ,"
their three rich notes formed a chord
of *glorious* complex harmony!
The vibration spun into existence
        building blocks of all that is
        and all that will be.

Sometimes we catch the echo, strain to hear
the thrum of God-sung harmonies,
the whisper of the whirling spheres.

In concert, someday, at the Throne,
we'll hear those pure, sweet, thrilling tones
        that once composed
        the world's first song.

THE LATEST NEWS

Ho, brave troubadour. Here halt.
Strike on your lute
a glittering chord.
Play for the lord,
join peasant's flute,
you, seated just above the salt.

Ho, sing out the news! We long
for songs of wars
won by our king.
Brave victories sing.
From foreign shores
(and battlefields,)
news comes in song.

Rhyme pattern: ABCCBA

NURSING HOME CHOIR
"How firm a foundation, ye saints . . ."
the nursing home residents sing.
Their voices, once —like their steps—so sure,
rise shaky and quavering.

"The soul that on Jesus doth lean . . ."
They know about leaning! These, once strong,
must now lean on others
for each little thing, all day long.

"I'll sanctify to thee thy deepest distress . . ."
Which distress? Death of spouse? Loss of home?
Or reduced to a bed and one drawer?
No visitors? Contrary roommate? Poor health?
Or just —that you can't lock your door?

*". . . I will not desert . . . I'll never,
no, never, no, never forsake."*
And their voices ring out, still shaky,
but firm—oh, so firm!—in their faith.

SONG OF PURPLE
I'll sing you of purple and its elegant shapes:
ovoidal eggplants and plums, global grapes.
I'll sing you of purple. And how does it feel?
Caress-able velvet, soft silk, rough chenille.
I'll sing you of purple, dawn-fragrant, dew-wet:
delphinium, iris, lilac, violet.
I'll whisper of purple, of secrets in stone
where amethysts, hidden in geodes, are grown.
Let's warble of purple, that glorious hue
worn proudly by grackles —and royalty too.
But the purple most royal, most lovely by far,
is the sky's evening wrap buttoned down by a star.

THOUGHTS WHILE LISTENING
to Piano Trio #2 in E Minor, Op. 67
written by Shostakovich to commemorate
a 1944 slaughter of Jews in Russia

"Sing," they said, "Sing us a song,
one of your songs of Zion,
songs of your homeland far away."
So we sang for our tormentors,
songs of home, of loss.
Voices broke, harp-strings snapped.
We hung our harps on willows
by the foreign stream.
*How can we sing the Lord's song
in the land of a stranger?*
Sweet songs of home—sung far from home—
became discordant sobs.
We, and our harps, are unstrung. *
# # # #
"Dance," they demanded. "Dance for us
one of your joyful Jewish dances."
And on the edge of our own graves
we danced.
"Dig, dance, and die," they mocked.
We dug, we danced, and
—shot by jeering soldiers—
we died. **
How could we dance on the lip of our graves?

O Lord God, receive our souls,
our dances, our songs.
Though far from home and *shalom*
we sing, we sob, we dance, we die.
Lord God, hear our cry!

* Psalm 137:2,3   ** Russia, c. 1944

MUSICAL SIMILITUDES

Spring afternoon,
two gifted musicians,
a program of Bach.
From a dark violin
(older than America)
notes like butterflies
float and flutter
now light and delicate
now vivid.
A change: passionate minor
swirls upward like birds
notes swoop, soar in a dance
choreographed by a master.
Swan-like, serene
the music flows, a quiet stream.
The organ's bass notes thrum below.
Then, like a whale
rising from great depths,
they surge upward
and explode in the air!

INVITATION TO THE CHOIR

How exciting! He's inviting
all of us to come and sing
in a coming Festival
honoring the King!
There will be a mighty choir
in antiphonal array,
plus a twenty-four voice chorus
gathered for that day.
A most unusual quartet
called "The Four Beasts" will present
their unearthly harmonies
climaxing the event.   *(continued)*

First, the Elders (twenty-four,
each with harp and incense) bring
their new song. Then, the angels,
swirling joyously, will sing.
We compose the other choir,
chosen ones from every race,
time, location—all creation!
Come and take your place.
Here's our music. We sing third,
echoing the angels' note.
What a thrilling chord of praise
pouring from each throat!
"Praise the One upon the Throne!
Praise the Lamb, once slain!"
Lift full-throated alleluias
to Messiah's name!
Hark! The Beasts' unearthly voices
speak a great Amen.
*(Breathless silence while the echoes
praise His name again.)*
What a privilege to be asked,
one and all, to come, to sing
in this glorious Festival
honoring our King!

*The twenty-four elders and the four living creatures fell down
and worshiped God, who was seated on the throne. And they
cried: Amen, Hallelujah!*
*Then a voice came from the throne, saying: Praise our God,
all you his servants, you who fear him, both small and great.
Then I heard what sounded like a great multitude, shouting:
Hallelujah!*
*For our Lord God Almighty reigns. Let us rejoice and be glad
and give him glory. . .. Blessed are those who are invited to the
wedding supper of the Lamb!* Revelation 19: 4-6

HYMN TO THE *LOGOS*

I sing your praise, O Thought expressed
and winged from God's great mind,
Creator of atoms and universe,
Lord of space and time.

As Word * made flesh, zygote-tiny
(compressed infinity)
helpless Almighty, babe new-born
yet older than eternity.

More wild and wonderful than fire – * *
that ancient foe and friend—
more powerful, more precise
than chisel in sculptor's hand.

As sculptor, You see possibilities
within my marble heart
and chip obscuring stone away,
to reveal Your living art.

I sing Your praise, *Logos* of God,
you Word *from* God, you *God-breathed* Word
who whispers love to love-starved hearts
and peace to this warring world.

* In the beginning was the Word [LOGOS},
and the Word was with God, and the Word was God.
He was with God in the beginning. John 1:1,2 NIV

* * Is not my <u>word</u> like a fire, like a hammer that shatters
stone?" Jeremiah 23:29 Moffat translation

CHAPTER 6. HOME IN THE COUNTRY

DAILY MIRACLES

Nothing is Everyday:
> light at a touch
> water at a wrist-flick
> food transformed to energy
> love translated to kindness
> passion that begets
> laughter that heals.

How can we call such things commonplace?
On every side there's barely elbow-room
> for all the miracles!

COAL-WARMED

Unused to ways of coal, we didn't bank
on how intense coal fires can get.
That winter midnight an August heat
awoke, alarmed, and drew us down
to find iron potbelly glowing cherry-red.
We learned: more air across the top,
less drawn up through the pile,
tempers wildfire tendencies.
Also, re-learned an ancient truth:
a fire's light and warmth
inscribes a family circle—
dogs included.

GROWING SEASON

A garden is a cause for praise
> not for the composted soil,
> the bulb,
> the garden glory,

but for the Giver of all life—
> even weeds, I guess. . .

A NEW LITANY

Thank you, Lord, for new beginnings:
    newly minted golden mornings
    first days of school, high school, college
    first job, new job, new position
    graduations, weddings, moving on
    first apartment, first owned home
    new bike, new car,
    new wife, new child.
As years rush by, still we begin anew:
    new roles, new responsibilities
    new challenges, new grandchild
    new things to learn, new friends to make
    new ways to fill the days after being
    newly retired.
Even to the close of life, we find:
    new mornings laced with love and coffee
    new aches and pains, new medicines
    new appreciation for thoughtfulness
    new eagerness to start the promised
    new life in a new Land
    with the same Lord who never changes
        and yet makes all things New.

NEW ENGLAND THRIFT

    Ringed round my garden
    rears a wall, each rock
      remembered well.
    My labor pried each loose
      from loam to lay it
    one by one and stone on stone,
    a useful wall and fertile field
    wrenched from rocky ground.

UN-NATURAL PARENTS

The cracked, brown-speckled egg
our dog stole from wild turkey's nest
contained your form, curled-up and damp.
Cracked eggs won't hatch, some claim,
but just the same I rigged a lamp
for warmth, and thought *We can try* . . .
  You hatched – a wobbly chick who gobbled
turkey mash and snuggled
under a feather duster
that you thought was Mom.
  Imprinted now on me,
you come to my clucking,
feast on crickets, ants and worms,
and follow me around the yard.
  But hard as we try,
we un-natural parents
(feather duster and I)
can't teach you how
to perch out of danger,
          talk turkey,
                    fear hunters,
                         or fly.

*This describes a friend's experience. The turkey grew
to adult-hood, but did not learn to fear hunters.*

CONDITIONED

Storm-bent till it forgot
how to stand erect,
the wind-warped tree
hunched defensively
even in a light breeze.

PROCESSIONAL

Cleopatra,
you deign
to enter doors I hold,
but pause mid-
way as if to show
which one is servant here.
And even when I nudge you on,
I seem to see, behind you, drawn
invisibly your train, perceived
but by the majesty
of your banner-tail.
Cleo, thou reincarnate queen
of sinuous step and haughty glance,
thou art a most
             imperious
                   cat!

REVELATION

I am lavender
cool blue reserve, pink propinquity
I am bread baking, homey stuff
to titillate taste buds and memories
I am cat, secretive, lazy
shall I/shall I not
I am willow, a wannabe dancer
rooted by traditional don'ts
I am spider, dangerous yet vulnerable
creating out of myself innate patterns
I am wind-chimes
music born of air and earth
I am autumn
conscious of winter coming . . . .

NATURE'S TRANQUILIZERS
On a country road where trees touch above,
they calm my spirit like a mother's hug.

When twittering birds (God's alarm clocks) greet
the dawn, I smile and yawn, and meet
the new day in peace.

When the water laps and slaps
the side of the anchored boat,
that peaceful sound gets my vote
as what I'd miss most.
Well,
come to think of it, there's a host
of good things I'd miss most.

FLASHBACK
Voices heard in another room,
bring memories of childhood sickroom
when I felt I was a universe apart,
as feverish malaise muddled me
into disorientation.

NIGHTMARE
Tiny Betsy thought the bathtub
had a monster's snout.
It tried to gulp poor Betsy
as the water gurgled out.
She plugged her foot into the drain.
The monster sucked her down.
Now Betsy's floating in the dark
somewhere beneath the town.

My little granddaughter loved this scary poem. !

WEARY PRAYER-WARRIOR
I found myself beside my bed
asleep (again!) upon my knees.
(I'm like those three beneath the trees
whom Christ had asked to pray.)
My idle hands need tasks to keep
this creeping sleep away.
Where Jacob wrestled God in prayer,
I mostly wrestle sleep.

MORNING ODYSSEY
I hear that siren call
and fain would stop my ears.
Pray, drag me thence
and bind me to the mast
of morn with lashings of
strong brew, before
I cast cold reason
overboard,
and crawl back into bed!

THE CLOCK
Relentless tyrant on the wall,
your seconds scurry,
minutes march, and
hours hustle by.
Dread warden of my day,
is Time your prisoner too?
You've set your chain on me
and locked me to your pace.
But someday He,
who is outside all Time,
will set me free!

THE IMPORTUNATE WIND

Away, west wind. The sash is fast
against your rude, insistent shake
and insubstantial fist. I won't
come out tonight. So—go away.

I've snugged my ears with muffling quilt
to dull your airy siren call.
So, west wind, whistle all you will,
I shall not listen. Go away.

The scudding clouds draw teasing veils
across the moon's astonished face.
No! Clouds may march at your behest,
but I refuse to. Go away!

Entice me not with memories
of other nights outdoors, blown here,
blown there, like milkweed fluff. Enough!
I won't come out. Please! Go away!

Oh well, perhaps this once I'll yield,
warm-sweater'd, to your chill embrace.
I'll join you for an evening lark
and revel in your gusts. I'll go.

Now, silly wind, don't tease and hold
the door. I'm up—now let me out.
Back off, or it's back to bed for me. . . .
I'll race you down the hill. Let's go!

S-S-S- SIBILENCE

If we could hear a word—familiar word—
as if it were an unlearned tongue,
ears hearing only sound, and mind
untrammeled by referent—
oh, could we guess that "s-s-sin"
and the implied, unspoken "dis-s-s-obedience"
held the hiss of danger,
the hiss of that stranger
who visited Eden uninvited
and left s-s-slithering on his belly.

Or consider another hissing word—
inverse of the first: across millennia
and up to Heaven's throne,
brilliant and breath-taking
as a comet's tail, glows Grace[s-s-s],
Christ's answer to our s-s-sin.

There, before the Judge we stand,
guilty, without excuse, but Grace[s-s-s],
the Living Word's efficacious word,
cancels our s-s-sin, raises banners of glory: Grace[s-s-s]
and Peace[s-s-s] and Bliss[s-s-s].

Ah yes! And then
like a punch in *solar plexus*
all air explodes in a
HHHallelujah!

RAINBOW

God set an arc of splintered light
for us to view through heaven's tears
for us to learn: even through grief
may glory gleam.

CHAPTER 7.   FAMILY LIFE

STONES OF REMEMBRANCE

Twelve stones gathered from a river bed
and stacked to remind in years to come,
"We passed through here dry-shod. *
Praise God!"

New diamond flashes on left hand,
catching and returning light
broken into bits of glory.
Love story.

Painted pebble has honored place
next to silver necklace, rings of gold:
truest of my jewels, this 3rd grade art:
Gift of heart.

Joshua 4:1-3,8,9

COME SHARE

Come share my pleasant stones,
come hear the story of each find,
admire the fool's gold shine,
with your thumb
rub the rough,
caress the smooth,
test the edge.
Come peer at whorls and ribs
of shellfish laid eons ago in stone.
Come marvel at God's ingenuity
and lavish hand. Come,
share my pleasant stones.

CHILD-LIKE FAITH

Lord,
may I see with fresh,
unaccustomed eyes—
with child-like eyes—
the wonders of Your Word
and the glories of Your creation.
Give me, I pray, a child's ear
for speech and meanings,
a child's curiosity for how and why
the world is like it is,
a child's love for those around me,
and a child's faith that my Father
is bigger than anybody's,
and when He holds my hand
and takes care of all my concerns,
nothing could be better than that.

CELEBRATION

Dance toward me, child,
on laughing feet,
and draw me up to join
your celebration.

COMMITTED

Learning to know you and be known,
means going, layer after layer,
deeper and deeper beneath the skin
that others know, into the strength
and sweetness at the heart. Sometimes—
as in peeling onions—we cry so hard
we can't see what we're doing. But
I don't give up onions for that reason.
Nor will I give up you.

THE UNSEEN

Across my electric alarm clock's face
is the daily reminder I pasted there once:
"Early will I praise Thee."
Or was it "Begin with God"?
I don't remember which.
The wooden plaque by the door says . . .
(now give me a minute,
it will come back to me.
It's from Psalms, I'm pretty sure . .)
And my bumper sticker.
I do remember how that goes:
"Wise men still seek Him."
But I'd forgotten it was there
until I washed the car.
All these fine mottos hung on
walls of house and car and soul
have dwindled to mere decorations
that, accustomed, I no longer see.
Forgive me, Lord. I've also grown
accustomed to Your grace.

WINDOW TO THE WORLD

Come climb the winding pie-wedge steps
to the big black bookcase in the hall.
The two top shelves were Mama's,
her Harvard Book Shelf Classics all
clad in mustard brown.
Some, like *Jamaica Inn,* I read, not sure
at twelve what it meant, but
(listening for her approach) quite sure
she didn't mean those books for me!
The lowest shelf held *My Book House,*
twelve favorites, bound in blue or green,
whose contents ranged from Mother Goose

(continued)

and Grimms to Homer. In between
were Beatrix Potters, robust Zane Greys,
Grace Livingston Hills, Carolyne Keene.
Our family kept its treasures free
for all to take. We'd choose a book,
descend the winding stairs,
curl up on a wide old windowsill,
and open up a world.

SLEEP SONG, A DUET

"It's late," you say. "Come to bed."
"I'm coming soon," I say. "You go ahead."
And so you do—up the stairs, into bed,
and into sleep, ahead of me.

I lay aside my book, do all
the little things of teeth and prayers,
then crawl in next to you.
Possessively, I tuck one arm
through yours, and slide into sleep . . .

Later I half-awake to find
we're nested, spoons in a drawer.
(My stomach warms your lower back
good as a heating pad, you've said.)

I clip us close, an arm across
your waist, unconscious symbol
of our marriage. You clamp my wrist
in place, your heart beneath my palm
drums a muffled, steady beat
to our duet. We breathe in unison,
a song of closeness, harmony.
Our song of sleep.

CHRISTMAS MORNING, DEJÀ VU

In these grandparent years,
four eager kids no longer fidget
by our bed, anticipating
lumpy Christmas stockings
and gift-wrapped mysteries to explore.
One might think we could ignore
the strident wake-up call of clock.
But no, an eager dog at bedside pleads,
"Let me out to sniff around. I need
to learn which midnight visitors
have wandered through the yard."
So up we get, and out he goes
to find (not sign of skunk, I hope) but—
reindeer tracks, do you suppose?

THE THOUGHTFUL HOST

Lord, may my hospitality
be, not in things I want to give,
but what my guest might really need:
no bustling, crowded, noisy feast
but just a snack, eaten in peace:
not entertainment long and late
but time to pray or meditate;
not guided tours, but little fuss,
laundry done, phone calls "on us."

Then may your servant leave my home
refreshed and strengthened for the next
well-meaning hosts who truly want
to treat God's servant royally,
when what he'd love to hear, perhaps,
is "Would you like to take a nap?"

BLESSINGS
on these common things:
warm showers, cold milk,
plaintive doves at dawn
and crickets' high-noon song,
the splat of huge raindrops on dry fields,
the giggle of a tickled child,
the comfort of my own bed,
a lighted window's welcome,
spring sun through unfurled leaves,
the whisper of first snow,
the moan of winter wind,
the bounty of my garden,
my cupboard's well-stocked shelves,
the hush of worship, shout of joy,
itch of healing, easing pain,
letters from home,
fragrant new-cut grass,
cicadas' August cacophony,
the right to worship unhindered,
and a Bible of my own.
I am so blessed!
Thank you, Lord.

INTRUDER
Brown-spotted, veined
and knuckle-gnarled—
whose hands, pray tell,
are these?
They can't belong
to one so young,
but they're sticking out
my sleeves.

SUBSTITUTES

My tastes have changed.
From years of sugar-free,
Splenda tastes "as-good-as."
From years of nearly skim,
whole milk seems rich as cream.
From years of "watch the fats"—
No! Some things are worth the risk!
Bring on real butter for my toast,
cream cheese for my—
      well, okay,
        for my celery.

THE SINGLES "GAME"

We seek relationships
in hectic ways,
indulging in
Trivial Pursuit,
knowing the Risk
of winner-take-all.
This is how
we Scrabble to avoid
the Pit of loneliness,
and Rook each other
without Scruples.
Twenty Questions
may be popped
over a glass of wine,
but never the one
Old Maids long to hear.

As for me, I have no Clue
how you really feel
without the Password:
I love you.

WAITING ROOM

In this place of dread, we wait,
immersed in introspection,
wholly focused on the aching tooth
or lump that warns of pain, disease,
or, perhaps, impending death.
Anxious, impatiently we wait
until our name is called.

"The doctor will see you now," they say,
and usher us through the door
into the presence of the one
we've waited here to see,
the one who knows our case.
We fear, yet long to "hand me over"
to the one whose skills we trust
to diagnose, correct, or cure.

At the threshold of death's door
we wait as well, dreading the step
into the unknown, yet—more—
hating the pain that brought us here.
How hard it is, so often, to pry loose
our clutch at life. Yet we must,
so our hands, reaching out,
and emptied
of temporal concerns,
may be filled with
greater gifts, better life,
and pain no more.

Once again, it is a matter
of fear overcome by trust.

ANTE-ROOM

This life is but an ante-room,
a vestibule in which we wait
until our summons to the King.
As each goes through the door,
those left behind may weep,
not knowing riches lie before
the passing one, and open arms
and unimagined joy.
Meanwhile, they wait within, secure,
and eager for <u>our</u> passage
through the door.

LOUISA'S PASSING

How strong is Life!
Tenaciously it clings
though sorrow, age or pain
bids it begone.
So long as God says, "Hold,"
it must hold on.

How fragile, life!
So little does it take
to break the fine-spun cord.
A clot, biopsy's report, a fall
shakes us awake
to our mortality,
reminds that we are all
bound "other-where beyond recall."

How strong. How fragile.
And how fine a gift.
But nearer river's bend, it flows—
how swift!

THE HOPE CHEST

Lovingly, hopefully, we lay away
within this chest, our very best,
against that Wedding Day.
It will, one day, be opened,
to bring forth, glorified,
much more than what was laid away,
transformed to be Christ's Bride.
A shell, an empty envelope
—no more—we lay away.
The precious essence God holds safe
until our Glory Day.

ENDS AND BEGINNINGS

If seeds were sentient,
would one, when buried, think,
"I guess this is the end."
Or would it sense within
a resurrection urge,
and, bursting from its shell,
know itself 'progenitor'
of vastly more beginnings
than one could ever tell?

METAMORPHOSIS

from dark cocoon-ment and mummy dreams . . .
endless, endlessly awaiting the call of light . . .
light long-absent creeps through a crack . . .
light that awakens a freedom thirst . . .
a thirst to claw your way out . . .
out of darkness to fulfillment, to light,
to a world of never-known *light-ness,*
and surging swelling resurrection,
to stretching rumpled
. . . . *wings?*

CHAPTER 8. LOVE AND MARRIAGE

GOLD-STRIKE

I deeded my next sixty years
or so, to you. They stretched
on our wedding day, horizon-like,
mysterious, endless, hiding
who-knows-what.
And then, like everybody else,
we minced our time into minutes,
squeezed it between deadlines,
shook it through the sieve of schedules.
Chunks of hard-won wisdom
and nuggets of memory remain—
the shining hours here and there,
some magic moments—more than most
have sifted from their marriage.

I'm convinced that we're the lucky ones,
to pan the sand of our lives and find
such gold, almost without trying!

STRETCH MARKS

The two-ness of our marriage stretched,
and stretched, and stretched again.
Fresh cords were formed and wrapped about,
supporting all the extra weight.
One by one by one by one, it shrank
to just us two once more. At first
our marriage sagged a bit, as if
it missed the fullness. But
elastic love snapped back to pull
it in around our two-ness once again.
Only—the stretch marks have remained,
reminding us how much we've gained.

LITTLE THINGS

It's little things, small irritants,
that quench the marriage spark:
  how to spend your Saturdays;
  "owl" hours versus "lark";
  what constitutes extravagance;
  lights left on, open drawers;
  a neatnik wed to a scatterer;
  and many (mini-) mores.
But also it's the little things
that fan our marriage flames:
  the unexpected gift or hug;
  the private jokes and names;
  cloaking faults, broadcasting praise;
  the little thoughtfulnesses;
  a foot massage or—ah!—backrubs
  are welcome as caresses!
It's up to us. We choose, you know,
how big these little things will grow.

THE FRUITFUL HOME

We labor here to build a home,
  God's Spirit, you, and me.
Love's walls stand guard against the world
  yet warm us cozily.
Peace roofs us over, points to God,
  and Joy throws wide the door.
Kindness cushions every task,
  and Patience pads the floor.
Each breath infuses with fresh Faith,
  cradled in Gentleness we rest
and feed on Self-control; our garments
  God's own Righteousness.
(Galatians 5:22,23)

ONE FLESH
Of dirt and breath
God formed one flesh.
One.
Only.
Lonely.
Then—creative surgery!—
of that one
two flesh were formed,
alike, and yet
not quite the same.
And two became
one flesh again.
Sin drove a wedge between.
Yet even now,
in God's grand scheme,
when two hearts mesh,
two bodies seem
to meld back into one,
once again.

BEYOND
Love sees the heart. The face, the form
may please the eye, or not.
The essential You reveals
itself but to the heart.
Your face I love, but should it change
by wrinkles, scars, disease,
love would not change, for I love you,
not just what my eye sees.
And so, though time's ungentle hand
obscures what first I knew,
I see beyond, and find myself
more deeply loving you.

LOVE LETTER

Why do I love thee?
Let me count the ways:
I love you because you drive slower
than conditions warrant,
just to ease my fears.
I love you because you never complain
about my weight.
I love you for your patience with me,
and for your sense of humor.
I love you because you are fun to be with,
and because we laugh together.
I love you because of your absolute
honesty and integrity and
sensitivity and ever-so-soft heart.
I love you because of the way
you encourage me
and tell me you are proud of me.
I love you for your tenderness,
your understanding,
(and several other qualities
too private to mention here.)
I'm sure I have left out
about a hundred other reasons, but
I'll tell you them some other time.
All my love, your wife

RECOGNITION

After sixty years I know
his steps from anyone's.
I don't know how I know.
Could be,
the rhythm matches
the rhythm of my heart.

HEART-ACHE

Lord, my heart hurts.
I see the pictures,
read the stories of abortions
multiplying to
incomprehensible proportions.
And I feel so sad: for the tiny ones
dismembered, known but to You;
for the nurses forced
by threatened job
to use their healing skills
for harm; for the mothers
ridding themselves, at once,
of 'excess baggage' and the chance
to know a toddler's guileless smile
and outstretched arms.
I hurt, Lord, for their hurt.
What can one person do?

Lord, my heart hurts.
The papers show the children—
lackluster-eyed, distended bellies,
twig-like arms—no food,
no water, no hope. And I
have too much—of all but hope.
I hope for their rescue, but
I fear that too is hopeless.
I hurt, Lord, for their hurt.
But what can one person do?

Lord, my heart hurts.
Molested toddlers,
kidnapped children,
teenaged prostitutes,
vacant-eyed druggies,

(continued)

purposeless adults,
the homeless and the destitute.
I hurt as I read about their plight.
But easy living wraps
its strangling arms around
my half-formed wish to help
and whispers, "What can one person do?"

Lord, Your heart hurts too.
That's why You came.
Long before the spear-thrust,
Your heart felt the ache to help.
You saw what one Person could do,
and did it. Now, help me see
what we two, You and I, can do.

FOCUS:
A CALL TO WORSHIP

Have you come to worship
the Lord of heaven and earth?
He is here.
Have you come with thanks
for blessings daily and eternal?
He is here.
Have you come with eager steps
to meet the One who loves you?
And did you speak to Him
when you came in?
He is here.
We are here. Let us speak to Him
and hear Him speak to us.

SHAPED FOR SONG

I watched as they shaped a Steinway,
heard the wood protest and groan
as workers strained to bend
the board against its will (or grain),
impose that graceful curve, then clamp
and glue and hold it there
relentlessly
until it yields.

A grand piano's shape is forced
upon it so. And then, from
conquered wood and
tensioned wire may
ripple, thunder,
flow, songs
that lift
to God
joyful
praise.

Shape me too, Lord,
even though it hurts,
so I can sing.

LOST TIME ?

Is all that past time really lost?
Or does God, on the Other Side
of His celestial hourglass
collect it to transform
(as He does to us)
into something fit
for eternity?

THE COMMUNICATOR

Go back

Go back
beyond words

Go back
beyond words
back to the mind's mystery

Go back   .
beyond words,
back to the mind's mystery
of synapses that snap together

Go back
beyond words
back to the mind's mystery
of synapses that snap together
into thoughts, words, commands

Go back
beyond words
back to the Mind and mystery
of synapses that snap together
into thoughts, words, commands,
like "Let There Be Light."
            And there was Light.

* * * * *

In the beginning was the Word . . .
and the Word was God. . . .
In Him was life, and that life
was the Light of men.
John 1:1,4

CHAPTER 9. ADVENT INSIGHTS

ANNUNCIATION WONDER
Do angels come like other folk
with steps that crush the grass
and even scuff up dust?
Or is it instantaneous—
a quiver in the air
like that one sees through candle flame,
or glimpse of unseen doors which yawn
as one steps through from there to here?

Have angels booming bourdon voices,
full-organ tones that quake the air?
And do they speak pure Aramaic,
or Hebrew with a Heaven brogue?

"Fear not," they say, but do they wonder
why these silly mortals tremble,
and maybe smile inside to think
that we on whom God's favor rests
should be afraid of such as they?

Do angels jostle for the job
of heavenly annunciator?
I shouldn't wonder if they'd shirk
this task of carrying good news
to fearful, slow-believing folk.

The angel . . . said, "Greetings, you who are highly favored!
The Lord is with you. . . Do not be afraid, Mary, you have
found favor with God. You will be with child and give birth to a
son, and you are to give him the name Jesus. . . . The holy one
to be born will be called the Son of God." Luke 1:28, 30, 35b

The Word became flesh and dwelt among us.

JOHN 1: 14

Through birth's channel
He entered our dimension,
    pitched a tent of flesh
    like that our souls inhabit,
      and subjected Himself
      to time and space.

THE JOURNEY

Those weary miles—did Mary ride
from Nazareth to Bethlehem?
Side-saddle, likely, not astride.
With no position easy—when
she feared her waters soon might surge,
the baby's head press to emerge—
she might dismount and walk a while.
Or huddle, rocking, on a stone,
arms cradled 'round her unborn Child,
wondering how she'd fare, alone,
with only Joseph to deliver,
far from home, far from Mother.
As spur to sometimes faltering will,
perhaps she thought of Gabriel
and what she'd said (so young, so bold)
in her acceptance speech: "Behold,
I am the handmaid of the Lord.
Be it according to thy word."
As Joseph helped her up to start again,
she'd sigh and say,
"How far is it to Bethlehem?"

INNKEEPER

It isn't that my heart is hard.
It's that the inn is full.
When every bed holds two or three
who've paid their coin, expecting rest,
who'll turn them out? Not me!
So what are reservations for?
My own bed even now
holds three tired travelers, and I—
my bed will be the floor.
The stable isn't very clean
nor tight against the wind,
but there at least is privacy,
a birthing place within,
not on the street as beggars must.
Necessity seems cruel.
It isn't that my heart is hard.
It's that the inn is full.

SOUNDS OF THE FIRST CHRISTMAS

In the hay-fragrant dark—
sounds of earth, sounds of birth:
panting, groans, grunts and moans
blend with dove's coo, rustling straw.

Sounds of birth, sounds of earth—
a sobbing breath of release underscores
a newborn's cry, protest at entering
a cold, new world.
Quiet outdoor sounds of earth—
the crackling fire, a sleepy bleat,
shifting weight off tired feet—
all suddenly overlaid
with heavenly song, unearthly light.

(continued)

The midnight sky glares bright
with flash of angel wings,
brighter yet than clearest day.
Sounds of heaven segue
to hurrying feet of men awe-struck
who go to seek, and finding, speak
their breathless, deathless tale
of angel messengers, of long-
awaited holy advent.
Two final sounds:
the ordinary earthly suck
and sigh of a milk-satisfied babe,
and rustling straw as Mother tucks
Him in, and murmurs to the baby king,
Hush now, my love, sleep in peace.

CHRISTMAS THANK-YOU NOTE

Your long-awaited Gift arrived
in excellent condition.
It was exactly what I needed.
Thank You with all my heart.

SWADDLED (I)

Wrap Him tightly, Joseph.
. . . Why? I don't know.
It's something women do—
wrap a babe in bands, wrap
so hands and feet can't move.
. . . What? Why not nail them?
Trust a carpenter to think of that!
Full freedom will come soon enough.
Just swaddle Him, Joseph,
and lay Him gently down.

(Compare to SWADDLED II on page 99)

FATHER SAYS

I'm learning from my father
how to guard the sheep.
  My father always says,
"Any fool can break a rule.
Now, son, when you're on watch,
don't watch the fire—
it dazzles your night sight—
nor talk so loud you miss the sound
of stalking wolf or bear, nor ever,
ever leave the sheep alone out there."
  But father never said what to do
when light from heaven dazzles
eyes accustomed to the dark,
nor how to listen for the wolves
while angels sing, nor if you stay
on watch when told to go.
  No, father never said.
But he, like me, like all of us, got up
and rushed to Bethlehem to see.
  You have to know, my father says,
when you're a fool
to *keep* a rule.

BORN TO THE PURPLE

Like all new babies, He held court
with mother's lap His throne.
Little fingers stretched to touch
earthly gifts the Magi brought
to Him who heaven's wealth had known.
"A king, not of this world." Not yet,
but one day all shall bow
before the King who governs now
in hearts of men, but then
He'll rule all things.
My heart, salute the King of kings!

BEHOLD, HIS GLORY

Wisely (they thought) they sought a king
in a palace, not a peasant's modest home.
But when their **G**lobal **P**ositioning **S**tar
pinpointed 'Here' they placed their gifts
and themselves in homage at His feet.
Apart from common lamps within
and uncommon astral glow without,
no nimbus crowned the Christ. Not yet.
But thirty years ahead,
three other awestruck men *
beheld that glory shining through
as if some shutters, long kept closed,
had opened and the light streamed out—
indwelling light, Shekinah glow
blazing through His flesh, a fire
that burned but not consumed.
Our Sun shines a glory all His own.
And we behold, bemused, as His
indwelling Glory fills us too,
and illuminates our human dust.

 * *Matthew 17:1-6*

THE WORD

In the beginning was—silence—
until the Word
sent reverberations rumbling
across the void in waves of meaning.
It crafted matter from nothingness,
stirred chaos into order, and set
the spheres to singing.
Then, like bell-strokes, the WORD tolled:

LET
    LIGHT
       BE !
AND   LIGHT   WAS !   (continued

That light was the light of men,
  but men preferred the dark,
  and dark, debasing words:
    lie, curse, vilify.
Words led to blows, to brother's death,
  to wars – a wicked harvest
  springing from a poisoned soil,
  sin heaped upon sin upon sin, upon sin.
Creation groaned
  beneath its awful weight.
Once more the Word sped across the void,
  to be embedded in a womb,
  nine months silent,
  until one night a newborn's wail
  was hushed with milk and lullabies.   *(continued next page)*

MARY'S WELCOME SONG

Little one who stretched and kicked
(and sometimes hic'd) beneath my heart,
precious boy, my pain and joy,
welcome to the world.
I whom you will call your mother,
he whom people call your father,
even shepherds from the hillside
gladly bid you welcome.
Did angels sing your farewell song?
There, heaven's riches were your own;
now your mother's breast is home,
and I bid you welcome.
My voice your choir, my lap your throne—
hush, my wee one, close your eyes.
Immanuel, God in disguise,
welcome to your world.

(THE WORD, continued)
Thirty quiet years went by. And then
once more the the Word was raised,
raising hackles, raising echoes of I AM:
I AM the Bread, the Life, the Way.
Hear me, all you with ears!
I AM
that
I AM.

APPOINTMENT

Have you walked Judea's roads?
Samaria's much the same: the heat
and dust, but add the burden of
dislike that flows from all you meet.
We'd not have picked this way to come,
but He, as though He'd prearranged
to meet someone, walked on.
He settled down by Jacob's well
and sent us into Sychar for
whatever we could buy to eat. We saw
a youngster ducking in a door
beneath his angry mother's arm;
a handsome woman balancing a jar
(her quickly hidden glance seemed, oddly, bold
and yet defensive); back of her, two men
whose knowing eyes assessed her swinging walk.
A shop with shutters dropped against the heat
provided us with olives, bread, and cheese.
Thus laden , we returned to eat
our lunch beside the well.
We found the Master talking earnestly
to her whom we had passed. But then
(continued)

He talks to all: a woman, child, or slave,
a master, Pharisee or publican
are interesting alike to Him.
Suddenly with lightened step and face
she left her jug and hurried back
to town. We made a place
to spread the food, and urged
him, "Master, take some time to eat."
We wondered what he meant
by saying He had 'other meat'?
Had someone brought Him lunch?
He often puzzles us,
and so He did that day
with talk of whitened harvest fields—
when harvest lay four months away. . .
Or did it? Crowds from Sychar came
and listened . . . and believed!
We learned that souls as well as wheat
can make up harvest sheaves.

* * * *

Teaching, preaching, loving, healing. Many followed
him. But even His disciples did not understand what his
destination was. Or why.

He kept telling them:
"The son of Man will be betrayed
to the chief priests and the teachers of the law.
They will condemn him to death
and will turn him over to the Gentiles
to be mocked and flogged and crucified."
Matthew 20:18, 19

On the road, going up to Jerusalem . . . Jesus was walking on
ahead of them, and . . . those who followed were fearful.
Mark 10:32

CHAPTER 10: PASSION WEEK

DESTINATION: JERUSALEM

He strides ahead.
His shoulders, squared and resolute,
shout His resolve; like flint, His face.
With eyes fixed on some private pain,
He sets the pace, unfaltering,
and strides ahead.

We trail behind, reluctantly.
To follow into certain death
with banners, shouts, and brandished spears
is one thing. But – unarmed and mute?
It has the smell of sacrifice
to us who lag behind.

We're fearful. Yet we follow Him
and sense the beat of dirge
that He alone can hear.
We follow Him from – what?
From habit? love? loyalty?
Perhaps it takes all three
to keep on going when you're scared
like me.

Then Jesus told them, "This very night you will all fall away on account of me, for it is written, "I will strike the shepherd, and the sheep of the flock will be scattered." Matthew 26:31

NIGHT IN GETHSEMANE

The evening meal of roasted lamb,
herbs, bread and wine is hours past.
Uncomprehending drowsy friends
doze as He prays in agony.

(continued

In shuddering obedience
He drains the bitter cup.
Torchlight, approaching,
glints on spears and swords
outside the garden's gate.

But Peter replied, "Lord, I am ready to go with you to prison and to death." Jesus answered, "I tell you, Peter, before the rooster crows today, you will deny three times that you know me." Luke 22:33,34

BESIDE THE FIRE

Smoke curls from glowing coals,
this cold spring night,
as tiny flickering flames
warm chilly hands
of those who wait
within this windy court.

Bored patience, idle talk, denying
none their meager warmth,
they've nothing else to do
except to notice who
else gathers round their fire.

Fear chills the heart as well
as wind can frost the fingers.
From which I shiver most
I cannot tell.

"What? Who, me?
One of his disciples? No.
I've told you twice already--
I do not know the man."

FOREBODING
Afraid, I fled down midnight streets,
as hunted conies seek a hole to hide.
Home isn't safe, and yet—
where else to go?
Behind my barricaded door, I crouch,
unnerved at footsteps in the street –
(. . . not coming here, thank God!)
O God! My Master,
like a common thief, arrested!
But – it's Passover.
They'll but imprison Him
until the Sabbath's passed.
By then old Nicodemus may find ways
to get our Lord released.
What charges could they lay?
His life is far beyond reproach.
They know—they watched him close enough!
Yes, surely this will come to naught . . .
And yet, he spoke tonight of treachery
and going where we could not come.
He *said* we'd scatter (as we have)
and leave him all alone.
I loathe my craven heart!
Yet here I cower, shuddering at steps,
despair devouring all hope.
Cold dawn can chill a fevered brain.
Perhaps Sanhedrin's cooler minds
may yet prevail.
. . . Will morning never come?

INDICTMENT
I am Pilate, governor, Roman.
I am a sword in an iron fist.
I am responsible to Caesar
for Pax Romana.

(continued)

I am NOT responsible
for this man's death.
See? My hands are clean.
I am a judge.
. . . . Yet by this single judgment
    I am forever judged.

THREE DAYS: Friday

It was a day just like today—
the sun came up, shone brightly,
birds sang, children playing underfoot
were scolded, shooed outdoors.
Mothers prepared meals, nursed babies,
while fathers took their offerings
(money gifts and lambs) to the Temple.
It was a day just like today,
but hot spring sun, pouring down
on the heads of those
who knelt to pound the nails,
made rainbows in the women's tears.
And then—high noon—the sun
hid its face at what they did to Him
who made the sun, the wood, the very rocks
that formed that fearsome hill.
Three hours—darkness reigned as if
the sun above conspired to blind
the eyes of those committing sacrilege.
As it does at night, birdsong ceased.
All creation seemed to hold its breath.
And then the earth shook violently
as that amazing *shout* rang out.
It is complete!

THERE STOOD BY THE CROSS

Because of duty, five stood there.
An officer and his four men
carried out their job,
one they'd done before
and would again.
Their job was hanging men to die.

Because of hate, some stood there.
They came to mock, to vilify
this influence they feared.
They had demanded, "Crucify!"
and then came to see it done.
All would be well—they hoped—
once he was gone.

Because of curiosity, some came.
They'd heard of this one who had healed
and, some said, even raised the dead.
Perhaps they'd see a miracle. At least,
they'd see the blood and horror,
have something to tell their friends.

Because of love, some stood there.
Helpless love had drawn them there
and kept them close. Their sympathy
could not reduce His pain, of course,
but just by being there, they hoped
to ease His broken heart.

By the cross I too must stand
and see the price He paid for me.

BEHOLD YOUR KING

Partners in crime hang side by side
(custom decreed) when crucified.
Yet here thieves flanked the Innocent.
  Positioned thus, it seemed to tell
the world that He, the center one,
was criminal as well,
even, possibly their chief.
  Nailed above each sufferer's head,
in three languages, three titles read:
    a thief – a king – a thief.
  A king? A joke, Pilate's plan
to mock the Jews who forced his hand.
      "Behold this bloody, helpless man."
Salt in a wound would have less sting
than the Roman gibe, "Behold your king!"
  But one recognized his majesty
and said, "Lord, please remember me
when you come into your kingdom hall."
  An unlikely convert—but aren't we all?
This thief, repentant, won the prize
of sins forgiven and Paradise!

Near the cross of Jesus stood his mother,
his mother's sister, Mary the wife of Clopas,
and Mary Magdalene. John 19:25

WE MARYS

Mary—
it's a common name. So common,
there were three of us who stood
that fateful day upon a hill
beneath a strangely darkening sky,
hearts raw and eyes wept dry.

(continued)

One of us knew gratitude
for healing (seven demons' worth); *
one knew the pain-pierced
mother's heart that Simeon foretold; **
and one, the wife of Clopas,
in her unobtrusive way
was his disciple, too.
Notorious, maternal, or obscure—
we Marys know a common love
and an uncommon Lord.
* *Mark 16:9* * * *Luke 2:53b*

A FOLLOWER

I followed Him from Galilee,
away from safety, home, and ease.
He counted my two sons among His men,
but that was only partly why
I followed Him.
I followed Jesus up that hill
and saw Him crucified, my arm
around His mother's waist, her tears
and mine intermingled for His pain.
I followed those who took Him down
to make a hasty burial—the sun, low
in the west, signaled Sabbath start.
The priests are strict: one must not break
their myriad rules. It matters less
to break a heart.

SHARED PAIN

Oh God! Each time
he pricks a finger, stubs a toe,
my heart contracts.
As Simeon foretold, I find it so.
Sharp as knives, I feel his pain.

(continued)

It is a mother's part
to bind up hurts
and kiss them well.
But some wounds strike too deep.
Some kisses taste of hell.

ODE TO ONE WHO TOOK MY PLACE

He bears the sin,
He feels the pain
I should have borne.
He wears the crown
I should have worn.
His love, made visible,
flows down His side.
It was for love He died.

. . . .

Note: There was a Joseph present at Jesus' birth (see page 86) as
well as at His death. Both men had the task and
the privilege to wrap the body of Jesus.

Joseph of Arimathea asked Pilate for the body of Jesus . . .
Nicodemus brought a mixture of myrrh and aloes . . .
Taking Jesus' body, the two of them wrapped it,
with the spices, in strips of linen.   John 19:38-40

SWADDLED (II)

Wrap Him tightly, Joseph.
Between the folds lay the myrrh
and aloes that we brought.
Indeed, we've got enough
for a King. But—
now our King is dead.
We bury Him we loved
and, with Him, bury all our hopes
of freedom from Roman rule.
(continued)

If God had some further plan,
it's surely one I cannot see.
Swaddle Him in bands,
and lay Him gently down.

BLUEPRINT

The Cross was not Plan B —
no makeshift hastily contrived
should Plan A go awry.
Designed before creation's dawn,
God's blueprint, drawn
in scrupulous detail,
was executed
according to plan,
right down to the last
nail.

JOSEPH: "I Tried . . . "

I gave Him my tomb.
What more could I do?
My voice in Council was weak,
shouted down when I tried
to counter their passion with reason.
I tried. Really, I tried.
What more could I do?
So I gave Him my tomb,
and spices enough to embalm a king.
I did what I could:
I gave Him my tomb.
But even the tomb was only a loan,
although I thought it was more.
I'll use it myself, but now I see:
any tomb is only a door.

The women . . . followed Joseph and saw the tomb and how his body was laid in it. Then they went home and prepared spices and perfumes. But they rested on the Sabbath in obedience to the commandment. Luke 23:55

THREE DAYS: Sabbath
It was a day just like today.
The sun shone brightly, yet
it still felt dark. Birds sang.
(We wondered how they could,
for our hearts held no song.)
Children played and laughed—
their carefree laughter seemed to grate.
This was the Sabbath, day of worship,
day of rest—but our souls were restless.
We bowed down—in pain, not prayer.
Our traitor hearts whispered,
    "Why worship? God let Him die."

THE ROCK
Like Jacob, pillowed on cold stone
my sleeping Savior lay
entombed behind
the stone-blocked door,
awaiting that Third Day.

haiku 12
Friday seemed final
pain, blood, desertion, darkness
but Sunday will come

When the Sabbath was over,
Mary Magdalene and Salome bought spices
so that they might go to anoint Jesus' body.
Mark 16:1

THREE DAYS: Resurrection
It was a day just like today.
The sun came up,
burned away the morning mist,
birds sang, families awoke,
stretched, yawned, got up—
only to stagger when earth convulsed
and groaned,
the sound of travail.

FROM WOMB . . .
I held Him—warm,
enveloped as He grew.
I held Him nine short months.
But when the time had come,
these fleshly walls could not retain
incarnate God,
and He burst forth—
Joy to the world!

. . . AND TOMB
I held Him—cold,
enshrouded in His death.
I held Him three long days.
But when His time had come,
my rocky walls could not restrain
the Lord of life,
so He burst forth—
Joy! Joy forever! Joy to the world!

MORNING ON CALVARY
Forgetting Friday's 'midnight-noon'
and early morning's trembling earth,
exultant bird-song greets the rising Son.
(continued)

The Gardener, whose heart
had sheathed a spear,
opens the gate again
to fellowship.

*On the first day of the week, very early in the morning,
the women took the spices they had prepared
and went to the tomb.* Luke 24:1

ANOTHER FOLLOWER

I followed, early, that same path
with the others who, as I,
were burdened to perform for Him
one final task of love.
Our fear was swallowed up in joy!
No need for spice or ointments now—
He lives! He lives! His body scarred,
yet new and incorruptible.
 (In that way, too, someday
   I'll follow Him.)
For now, it is enough to know
He leads—indeed, He *is* the Way,
and so I can't be lost. For that,
and love, but mostly love,
I follow Him.

SUNRISE SERVICE

The faithful, shivering, come
as morning mist in gauzy drifts
enshrouds the trees and graves.
Our newly-risen Sun,
dispelling haze, invites the gaze,
accepts the touch on wounded feet.
My Lord and God!
Accept my worship and my praise!

THE SON'S FOREVER DAY
It was a day like no other,
  never before,
    never again the same.
A day when all was changed,
  a day of joy,
    of celebration,
      of incredulity,
        of Resurrection!
                    Today the sun may shine, or not –
                      the Son of God forever shines
                      His light into receptive hearts.
                      Henceforth, *every* morning
                        is Easter morning!

*"Behold, I am coming soon! My reward is with me,
and I will give to everyone according to what he has done.
I am the Alpha and the Omega, the First and the Last,
the Beginning and the End. . . . I am the Root and the
Offspring of David, and the bright Morning Star. . . . Yes,
I am coming soon."* Revelation 22:12,13,16,20

O HAPPY DAY
Fireworks,
  ticker tape parades,
    dancing, shouts and tears
      suffice for life's
        festivities.
But at His shout, at His return,
joy inexpressible and full of glory
  will burst the bonds of gravity,
    and we shall dance,
      enraptured,
        in the air!

The End

OTHER BOOKS
BY JANA CARMAN

In the Beginning:
Genesis People Speak

Wilderness Trek:
Exodus Thru Sinai to Grace

Immanuel:
God in Disguise

Her Hostage Heart
(A Christian Romance)

Stella !
My Life a Dream Come True
by
Stella Baum with Jana Carman

The above books are available on Amazon and for Kindle

People of Faith
A Collection of Monologues, Sketches,
and Dramatic Poetry
Lillenas Publishing Company
(This book is out of print but can be
found occasionally on Amazon as a used book)

ENDORSEMENTS

Leo Thorne writes:

I appreciated the pre-publication opportunity to read Jana's book "Of Roots and Wings and Heart-felt Things." By drawing on her keen observations as a person living close to nature and God, Jana really does "farm the air," as she said in her poem "Madam Spider."

Once I began reading it, I could not put it down. It is indeed A Good Read. (*See the back cover for the rest of his endorsement.*)

Rev. Leo S. Thorne, Ph.D., author, poet, pastor, former tenured Associate Professor at Fairleigh Dickinson University, editor, and radio host of The Poet's Corner.

Shirley Stevens writes:

In her book of poetry, Jana Carman takes us through the seasons, those in the natural year and those in our lifetime, demonstrating the same legerdemain she uses in playing the piano and organ. She adds deft touches through her images and diction. Describing Spring initially as genteel, she adds raucous tulips. The spent storm grumbles in the distance. Jana also surprises us with winter fireflies.

When Jana writes about interpreters for the deaf, she calls their rhythm "blank verse in motion" and adds their "silent hallelujahs and unspoken benedictions."

She reminds us to find blessings in common things: warm showers, cold milk, "plaintive doves at dawn . . . crickets' high-noon song."

In her very moving poem written in response to Shostakovich's Piano Trio #2 in E Minor, Op. 67, the Jewish victims slaughtered in Russia in 1944 are speaking to God as they sob, dance, and die "on the lip of their graves."

I heartily endorse Jana Carman's gift of poetry.

Shirley Stevens, teacher, mentor, poet

Contents, expanded --

POEM INDEX
Page number follows

Made in the USA
Middletown, DE
20 May 2023

30616408R00076